St. Patrick's Day

This holiday commemorates the patron saint of Ireland, Bishop Patrick, who in the year A.D. 432 left his home in France to bring Christianity to Ireland. Tradition says that Patrick drove the snakes from Ireland, but biologists say there were none in the country at the time. Shamrocks are associated with St. Patrick's Day because the Bishop reportedly used the three leaves to illustrate the Trinity.

The holiday, March 17, is marked by parades in cities across the United States. The largest of these, held since 1762, is in New York City and draws more than one million spectators each year. In Ireland, it is a religious holiday similar to Christmas and Easter. The parades and shamrocks are provided primarily for tourists.

Related Activities

- Discuss the country of Ireland and the history of St. Patrick. For books to read aloud, see the *Literature, Poetry, Songs, and Technology Connections.* Use the activity *"The Republic of Ireland"* provided in this booklet.

- In conjunction with St. Patrick's Day, you may wish to designate a "Green Day" for students. Use some or all of the following activities to make that day special.

  1. Ask your students to wear green clothing. See how many shades of green they can wear. Group them according to who is wearing a green shirt, green socks, green shoes, etc.

  2. Have children brainstorm a list of green foods. Write them in alphabetical order on the chalkboard. Then take a poll to find out which green foods they like most. You may wish to have students use the data from the poll to make bar graphs.

  3. Make a class book showing pictures of things that are green. Collect color pictures from magazines, advertisements, and catalogs. As an alternative, have students use the green pictures to create a class collage.

  4. Divide the class into small groups. Have students brainstorm a list of words that begin with the "gr" blend, such as "great" and "grip". Then have them think of rhyming words for each word on the list.

  5. Give each child a paper shamrock or have students make the shamrock pins described in this booklet. Discuss the Irish custom for St. Patrick's Day, called "the wearing of the green." This ancient custom originated as an important symbol of springtime and hope. Talk about how shamrocks also symbolize good luck. Brainstorm a list of other items that symbolize good luck, such as a horseshoe or a rabbit's foot.

  6. Enjoy a snack of green bagels or green muffins and green milk. Pistachio pudding also works well for a treat. **Warning:** Be sure to ask parents if their children have any food allergies or dietary restrictions before serving any snacks.

- Invite students to march to "Macnamara's Band" by Shamus O'Connor (Vogel Music Co., Inc., 1917). This music has a strong marching rhythm, and the lyrics mention drums, cymbals, and a flute. If possible, provide drums, cymbals, and flutes for students to use while they are marching. Students can pantomime playing the instruments if real ones are not available.

St. Patrick's Day *(cont.)*

Related Activities *(cont.)*

- Obtain recordings of traditional Irish music from your school or public library. You may wish to use these recordings as background music while students work on the activities described in this booklet.

- Have students dance an Irish jig to music. Technically, a jig is a lively dance done in triple time. However, you can teach students a few simple steps before you begin. These are not official steps for a jig; however, your students should get a great deal of enjoyment from this dance. Modify as necessary for young children.

  1. Jump up and down from one foot to the other, pulling first the right knee up while the left foot is down and then vice versa. Repeat this several times.

  2. Shuffle the right foot forward and back three times. Then switch, and shuffle the left foot three times. Switch back and forth several times.

  3. Swing the right foot across the left leg. Bring it back quickly and then swing the left foot across the right and back. Repeat this several times as quickly as possible.

  4. Invite students to come up with a few steps of their own.

     When students have learned the steps, have them stand in a circle, giving one another plenty of room to move. To begin, everyone should stand with arms akimbo. If possible, play some upbeat Irish music. Otherwise, any music with a lively beat will do. Lead students in some steps, using a random order. Do not worry about the technicalities of triple time. Just remind students that they should quickly move their feet to the music. After awhile, encourage students to improvise their own steps.

- Provide the class with several books about Ireland. Discuss important facts about the people, farming, life in the cities and countryside, and St. Patrick. Invite students to design travel brochures encouraging people to visit Ireland. They may wish to use the flag from *The Republic of Ireland* activity found in this book.

- Talk about the Irish lore of the mischievous leprechaun. Create a leprechaun marionette, using the directions and pattern provided in this booklet. Invite students to name the leprechaun. Display the marionette in the classroom as your lucky mascot during March. It's especially fun if the leprechaun (with a little help from you) plays harmless pranks during the night, such as hiding the reading books or moving desks around the classroom.

- Have students make individual leprechaun marionettes, using the directions and pattern found in this booklet. Then divide the class into cooperative learning groups. Ask students to manipulate their marionettes while telling leprechaun stories to their groups. Remind students that the stories can either be made up or a retelling of stories they have heard or read.

St. Patrick's Day *(cont.)*

Related Activities *(cont.)*

- Make some lucky headbands for students to wear on St. Patrick's Day. Cut 2" (5 cm) strips of white or yellow tagboard that are long enough to go around a child's head. Staple the strips to make the headbands. Then have each student cut out three green shamrocks. Ask students to write one wish on each shamrock. Tell them to glue the shamrocks onto the headband. If desired, a hot glue gun may be used to add pennies to each headband.

- Make a large butcher paper rainbow to place on a bulletin board. Laminate the rainbow before displaying it. Fill a jar with pennies or candy coins. Ask students to pretend that the jar is a pot filled with gold coins. Place the pot at one end of the bulletin board rainbow. Have students estimate how many coins are in the "pot of gold." Use an overhead marker to write students' estimates on the rainbow. Ask students to check their estimates by grouping the pennies or candy coins by tens and counting them. Have students find the differences between their estimates and the actual number of coins.

- Have students enjoy a treasure hunt, using the coins from the activity described above. Before students arrive, hide some or all of the coins in the classroom. After students arrive, divide the class into teams. Let the teams work together to find as many coins as they can. You may wish to put a time limit on the treasure hunt. When all of the coins have been located or time is up, have students group the coins by fives or tens. Have them add to determine the total number. Then ask them to estimate the total weight of the coins. Help them check the weight, using a scale. Have them find the difference between their estimate and the actual weight of the coins.

Bibliography

Books

Barth, Edna. *Shamrocks, Harps, and Shillelaghs: The Story of St. Patrick's Day Symbols*. Clarion, 1977.

dePaola, Tomie. *Jamie O'Rourke and the Big Potato*. Scholastic, 1992.

dePaola, Tomie. *Patrick, Patron Saint of Ireland*. Holiday, 1992.

John, Joyce, illus. *The Leprechaun's Treasure*. Nystrom, 1992.

Markham, Marion M. *St. Patrick's Day Shamrock Mystery*. Houghton, 1995.

Shute, Linda. *Clever Tom and the Leprechaun*. Scholastic, 1988.

Poetry

Livingston, Myra Cohn. "Saint Patrick's Day" from *Celebrations*. Scholastic, 1985.

Technology

Holiday Facts & Fun: St. Patrick's Day. (Video); 10 min. Charles Clark Co., Inc., 4540 Preslyn Drive, Raleigh, NC, 27616; 1-800-247-7009.

The Republic of Ireland

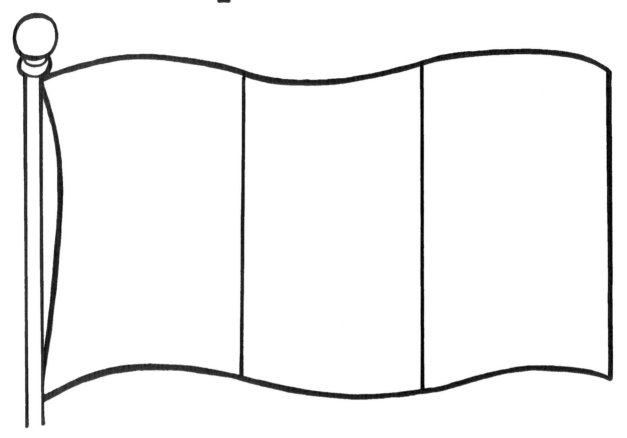

Look at the flag shown above. It is the Republic of Ireland's flag. Color the left section green, the center section white, and the right section orange.

Now read the following sentences to learn some facts about the Republic of Ireland.

1. The Republic of Ircland is on an island with Northern Ireland.
2. The capital city is Dublin.
3. Two languages, English and Gaelic, are taught in schools.
4. Many of the people in the country are farmers.
5. The government is a democracy with an elected president.
6. The major religion is Catholicism.
7. Patrick is the patron saint of Ireland.
8. Patrick helped teach people to read and write.
9. St. Patrick feast day, March 17, is a national holiday in Ireland.

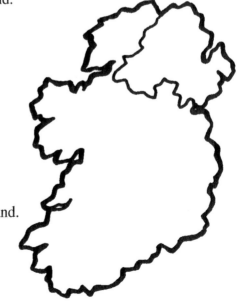

Shamrock Leaves

Reproduce the patterns shown below on green cardstock. Have students cut out the patterns and glue them together as shown. Invite students to decorate their shamrocks with glitter or sequins. After the glue has dried, display the shamrocks in the classroom.

Hidden Clovers

There are four four-leafed clovers in this field. Help the leprechaun find them. Color them green.
Then draw and color four more gold coins in the leprechaun's pot.

Pots of Gold

There are coins in each pot. Write numbers on the coins so they add up to equal the total shown below each pot of gold. Use 25¢ (quarter), 10¢ (dime), 5¢ (nickel), and 1¢ (penny).

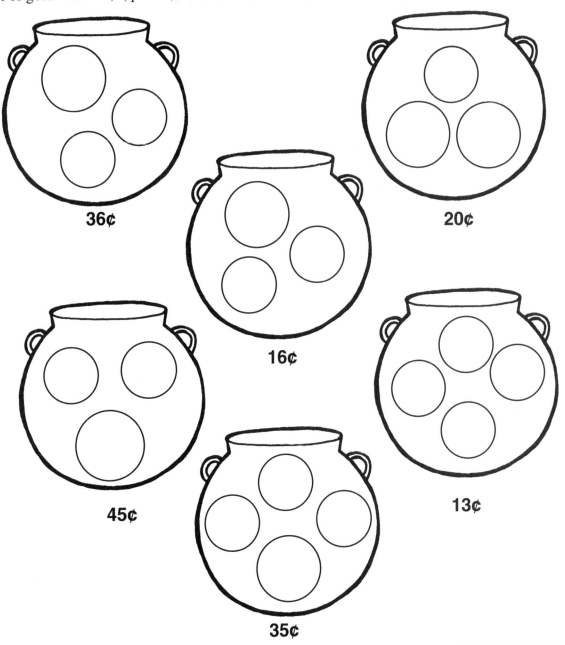

36¢

20¢

16¢

45¢

13¢

35¢

Answer Key

Fold up or cover the following answers before reproducing this page.

36¢ = 25¢, 10¢, 1¢   20¢ = 10¢, 5¢, 5¢   16¢ = 10¢, 5¢, 1¢

45¢ = 25¢, 10¢, 10¢   13¢ = 10¢, 1¢, 1¢, 1¢   35¢ = 10¢, 10¢, 10¢, 5¢

Tasty Potato Soup

Students may enjoy making and eating potato soup. Be sure to ask parents if their children have any food allergies or dietary restrictions before serving the soup.

Ingredients:

9 potatoes, peeled and diced

6 stalks of celery, sliced

2 small onions, chopped

3 cups (750 mL) water

2 teaspoons (10 mL) salt

3 chicken bullion cubes dissolved in ¹/₂ cup (125 mL) cup boiling water

6 cups (about 1.5 L) milk

¹/₂ cup (125 mL) flour

1 stick margarine or butter

Directions:

Combine the potatoes, celery, onions, water, and seasonings in a large pan. Bring these ingredients to a boil. Cover the pan and cook the mixture until it is tender, about 30 minutes. In a bowl, combine a small amount of milk and flour. Stir this mixture until it is smooth. Add it and the rest of milk to the ingredients in the pan. Stir in the butter. Cook over a medium heat, stirring constantly, until the soup thickens.

This recipe makes about 3 quarts (3 L) of soup or 24 ¹/₂-cup (125 mL) servings. Serve the soup in Styrofoam cups.

Extended Activities:

- Potatoes are one of Ireland's major agricultural products. Grow sweet potatoes in class by placing them in clear drinking glasses or plastic cups. Poke 3 or 4 toothpicks about halfway into the middle of each potato so that the toothpicks rest on the rim of the glass or cup. Place the potato in the container and add enough water to reach the bottom of the potato. Watch the potato plants grow.

- Discuss the different ways potatoes are cooked and eaten. Have students vote for their favorite ways to eat potatoes. Then have them make bar graphs showing their preferences.

Ways to Eat Potatoes	Number of Votes
Baked	
Fried	
Mashed	
Boiled	

- Cut a potato in half. Draw an outline of a shamrock on the cut surface of each half. Carve away some of the potato around each shamrock shape. Pour some green paint onto a plate. Place the cut potatoes and paint in an art center. Allow students to dip the potatoes into the paint and stamp the shamrock prints onto white construction paper.

Pop-up Card

For St. Patrick's Day, make a pop-up card to send to a friend or relative.

Materials for Each Pop-up Card:

- two 8 ½" x 11" (21 cm x 28 cm) pieces of construction paper
- crayons
- scissors
- pencil
- ruler
- glue
- one of the patterns from the next page
- envelope with a postage stamp
- address of the person to whom the card will be mailed

Directions:

1. Fold one piece of construction paper in half lengthwise.
2. Measure and mark 2 ¾" (7 cm) from each side along the fold. Cut 2 ¾" (7 cm) slits at the marks.
3. Push the cut area inside out and crease it to form the pop-up section
4. Glue the other piece of construction paper to the back, avoiding the pop-up section.
5. Color and cut out one of the patterns shown on the next page.
6. Glue the pattern onto the pop-up section of the card.
7. Sign your name.
8. Fold the card and put it in an envelope. Seal and address the envelope. Then place a postage stamp on it.

Pop-up Card Patterns

Green Riddles

Read and answer the riddles below. Remember that the answers are things that are green.

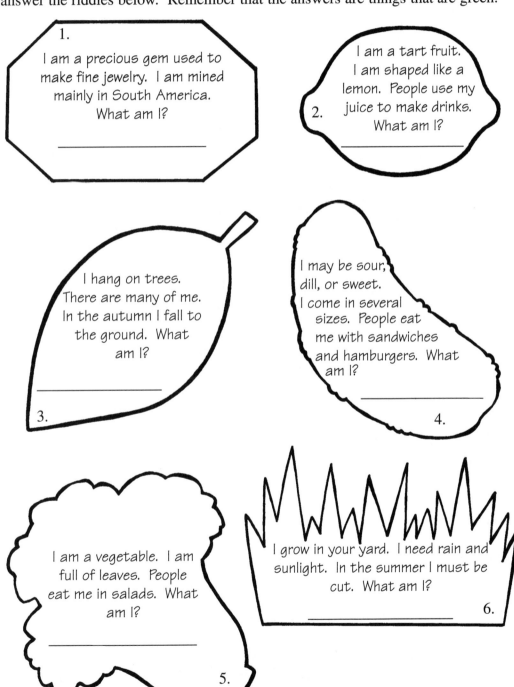

1.
I am a precious gem used to make fine jewelry. I am mined mainly in South America. What am I?

_____

2.
I am a tart fruit. I am shaped like a lemon. People use my juice to make drinks. What am I?

_____

3.
I hang on trees. There are many of me. In the autumn I fall to the ground. What am I?

_____

4.
I may be sour, dill, or sweet. I come in several sizes. People eat me with sandwiches and hamburgers. What am I?

_____

5.
I am a vegetable. I am full of leaves. People eat me in salads. What am I?

_____

6.
I grow in your yard. I need rain and sunlight. In the summer I must be cut. What am I?

_____

Shamrock Pin

Show students how to make a shamrock pin. Then invite them to make their own.

Materials for Each Pin:

- shamrock pattern (shown below)
- 3" (8 cm) square of green tagboard
- pencil
- scissors
- green glitter
- glue stick
- transparent tape
- small safety pin

Directions:

1. Place the shamrock pattern on the tagboard square.

2. Use a pencil to trace around the pattern.

3. Cut out the shamrock pattern from the tagboard.

4. Trace around the edge of the shamrock with the glue stick.

5. Sprinkle the green glitter onto the glue to make a sparkling border. Shake off any excess glitter.

6. Tape the back of the safety pin onto the back of the shamrock.

7. Put on the shamrock pin.

Leprechaun Marionette

Use the directions below and the pattern on the next page to make leprechaun marionettes.

Materials for each marionette: pattern from the next page, four copies of the strips shown at the bottom of this page, white cardstock or stiff paper, paper towel tube, 11' (4 m) piece of string or yarn, glue or tape, scissors, hole punch, markers or crayons

Directions:

1. Use white cardstock to reproduce the pattern on the next page. Color the pattern pieces and cut them out.

2. Fold over the head. Then punch a hole in the hat.

3. Roll the body into a tube shape. Fold in the tab. Fasten the back together with tape or glue.

4. Make eight strips, using the two patterns shown at the bottom of this page. Glue or tape together two strips, end to end, for each arm and leg. If glue is used, allow it to dry. Accordion-fold the strips to make two legs and two arms.

5. Punch holes in the hands and shoes. Glue or tape them to the ends of the arms and legs. Be sure to place the left hand and shoe on the left side and the right hand and shoe on the right side.

6. Use tape or glue to attach the face to the front of the body and the neck inside the back of the body. Attach the arms and legs to the body with tape or glue.

7. Cut a 15" (38 cm) length of string. Tie one end of it around the middle of the paper towel tube and attach the other end to the leprechaun's hat.

8. Cut a 3' (1 m) length of string. Tie one end of the string onto one end of the paper towel tube. Attach the other end of the string to the leprechaun's left shoe. Cut another 3' (1 m) length of string and do the same for the right shoe. Be sure to tie this string to the same end of the paper towel tube as the left foot.

9. Cut an 18" (46 cm) length of string. Tie one end of the string onto the unused end of the paper towel tube. Attach the other end of the string to the leprechaun's left hand. Cut another 18" (46 cm) length of string and do the same for the right hand. Be sure to tie this string to the same end of the paper towel tube as the left hand.

10. Manipulate the marionette by raising and lowering the strings with the paper towel tube.

Leprechaun Marionette Pattern

Search for Handmade Gold

Materials:

- white glue
- gold glitter
- paper
  or pen

- reclosable plastic bag
- small, smooth rock
- pencil

Directions:

1. Pour some gold glitter into the plastic bag.

2. Smear glue all over the rock.

3. While the glue is still wet, place the rock in the plastic bag. Seal the top of the bag.

4. Shake the bag until the rock is covered with the glitter.

5. Open the bag, but leave the rock inside of it. Allow the glue to dry. Remove the rock after the glue has dried.

6. Hide your gold nugget in the classroom or on the school grounds, depending on your teacher's directions. Do not tell anyone where your nugget is.

7. On a piece of paper, write specific directions telling how to find your gold nugget.

8. After writing your directions, choose a partner. Be sure your partner has hidden his/her gold nugget and written directions for how to find it.

9. Trade directions with your partner. Search for each other's gold nugget.

Limericks

Limericks are short, traditional Irish poems that often have an amusing ending. They are composed of five lines, with the last word of each line rhyming in an *a-a-b-b-a* rhyme scheme.

For example:

> There once was a young man from Kew
> Who found a dead mouse in his stew.
> Said the waiter, "Don't shout
> Or wave it about,
> Or the rest will be wanting one, too!"

Now try completing the limericks below. Fill in the ending rhyme(s) on the blank lines provided, making sure that the finished limericks follow the *a-a-b-b-a* rhyme scheme.

There was an old man with a beard,
Who said, "It's just as I feared!
Two owls and a hen,
Four larks and a wren
Have all built their nests in my _____."
by Edward Lear   (1)

There was a young maid who asked, "Why
Can't I look in my ear with my _____?
                                        (2)
If I give my mind to it,
I'm sure I can do it,
You never can tell 'til you _____."
by Edward Lear   (3)

There once was a boy named O'Toole,
Who didn't act smart when at _____.
He tried to read _____   (4)
But got dirty looks, (5)
And he grew up to be quite a _____.
                                        (6)

Extended Activity: On a separate piece of paper, try writing a few limericks of your own.

- -

Answer Key: (1) beard (2) eye (3) try (4) school (5) books (6) fool

Teacher Instructions: Fold at dotted line before copying in order to hide Answer Key.